CHUCK YEAGER GOES *SUPERSONIC*

AN ACTION-PACKED, TRUE FLYING ADVENTURE

by ALAN W. BIERMANN

Illustrated by YAEJIN LIM

CHAPEL HILL, NORTH CAROLINA

For Alice, Jennifer, David, Isabel, Sophia, David, and Elizabeth. A. W. B.

To Alexey, mother, grandparents, Slava, Irina and Natasha.
In admiration and gratitude. Y. L.

Text Copyright © 2011, 2012 by Alan W. Biermann
Illustrations Copyright © 2012 by Yaejin Lim
First edition 2013

Some photos on the Internet were used as guides for certain illustrations: Page 11, The Museum
of Flight, Seattle, Washington; pages 23 and 35, NASA web site; pages 39 and 41, Smithsonian
National Air and Space Museum; pages 43 and 44, cockpits, rocket engine, propeller and engine,
NASA web sites; jet engine, Wikipedia.

Design and book production by Julia Gignoux, Freedom Hill Design and Book Production
Illustrated by Yaejin Lim.

ISBN-13: 978-1480276321   ISBN-10: 1480276324

Chapter One ★ A Life of Adventure

Chuck Yeager loved to fly airplanes. He loved to fly high. He loved to fly fast. He loved to do loops and rolls. This is the story of how he became a national hero.

Life was not easy growing up in Hamlin, West Virginia in the hard times of the 1930s. Chuck's family counted on him for help, especially when his father was at work. Chuck and his older brother Roy planted and picked the vegetables on the land behind their house. They milked cows, scattered corn for the clucking chickens, and fed the hogs.

4

But when chores ended, Chuck went off into the woodlands around his home with his brother and friends, ready for wild adventures. They explored new paths and climbed trees. They loved swinging from vines out over their swimming hole and dropping into the water. Chuck also hunted in the woods, often bringing home meat that his mom could cook for dinner.

As he was growing up, he began to help his dad in the gas fields. His dad worked for a company that drew gas from underground to be sold for fuel. Chuck learned how the machines worked and he became an able mechanic. He was learning skills that he would need when he became a pilot.

Chuck finished high school just as World War II was beginning. He might have gone to college, but Chuck learned best by doing and he loved adventure. So he signed up for pilot training in the Army. Then he went to England to fight the war. He was an outstanding fighter pilot and a hero in combat. He flew so well that he earned the rank of Captain.

Chapter Two ★ Flying in the Air Force

When the war was over, Chuck became a maintenance officer in the U. S. Air Force at a base near Dayton, Ohio. His commander, Colonel Boyd, gave him his orders. Chuck stood at attention and answered "Yes Sir."

One day, the colonel ordered Chuck to test fly a new jet fighter, a P-59. It was the very first jet fighter in the U. S. Air Force. Chuck saw that this new airplane had no propeller on the front like others. He studied the new jet engines to see how they worked. He wanted to have a plan if something went wrong.

Finally, he was ready to fly. He started the engines and steered the plane onto the airstrip. He turned on full power for takeoff. The jet engines screamed. The airplane raced down the runway. Chuck pulled back on the control stick. The plane climbed into the air.

Chuck tested the plane by doing some climbs and dives and sharp turns. Suddenly he noticed a plane above him high in the sky. A P-38 fighter plane was diving towards him. What was this crazy pilot doing? Usually the other pilots were serious, but this one flew like one of his buddies from the war. That pilot was going to pretend to shoot Chuck's plane down. Chuck knew it was all in fun and he knew how to fight back.

He turned his plane hard to get away so that he'd get into a position to shoot the other guy down. He pulled his plane into a steep climb, flying straight up. The enemy plane followed just behind him. Then Chuck's plane stopped in midair and started falling. Both planes dove downward. Now they were going after each other near the ground. This chasing and chasing was called a dogfight.

Then, with engines screaming and planes smoking, a radio call came in from the other pilot. Maybe this wild flying was becoming too risky. The two pilots agreed to end their playful fight and land their planes.

Chuck wanted to meet this good flier. He walked over to the parked P–38 and shook hands with the pilot. His new friend was Bob Hoover. They laughed about their wild dogfight and knew they would enjoy many more.

Then they talked for a while about flying in the Air Force.

One day Colonel Boyd asked
Chuck and Bob to fly two of the
newest Air Force jets in an air
show. He knew they could put on
a great performance. They started
out with a joke asking two men to
stand behind the two jets. The men
held flames up to the tail pipes and
pretended to light the fires of the jet
engines. The crowd loved it.

Then the two pilots took off in their planes and climbed into the sky. They dove fast and the crowd cheered with excitement. The roar of the engines shook the earth. They pulled up sharply and climbed high again. Smoke streamed out from their planes. After doing many tricks, they ended their show. They landed their planes and waved to the people. Chuck and Bob flew many great air shows.

One time on their way home, Chuck's plane had engine trouble. But because of his knowledge of engines, he was able to keep it running and they made it back safely. Chuck was happy he had studied jet engines carefully. Bob saw once again that his friend was a great flier.

Chapter Three ⭐ Test Pilot School

Colonel Boyd knew that Chuck was a very unusual pilot. He had excellent flying abilities and a good feeling for the machinery of the planes. The Colonel decided that Chuck could do more advanced flying if he had some special training.

This was an exciting time for people who were flying fighter planes. The Air Force was working on a plan to fly planes faster than the speed of sound. When flying at high altitude, they would have to fly faster than 660 miles per hour. But there would be problems along the way.

Colonel Boyd asked Chuck if he would like to go to test pilot school. Chuck was worried because he had never gone to college. He had only finished high school. Test pilot school could be very hard. Most of the other students would have college educations. Colonel Boyd said that Chuck would do fine. So Chuck began test pilot school. He was happy that Bob would be there also.

The flight school teacher
began to talk about flying and speed and
climb and drag and angles. He went on and on and
showed a lot of graphs and numbers that were hard to understand.

Chuck was worried. The lessons were really hard. But he noticed one
student who seemed to understand everything. His name was Jack Ridley.
Chuck asked him some questions and Jack explained a few of the graphs
and numbers. This helped Chuck very much and from then on, he talked
to Jack a lot.

The flight school students also had to do flying tests. One day Chuck took off to do some speed tests with his instructor in the back. Suddenly there was a crashing sound in the engine. The whole airplane started shaking. Chuck knew he would have to land quickly.

He saw a farm below and aimed his smoking plane for a big field. Chuck stayed cool. He and his instructor tightened their seat belts and prepared for a hard landing.

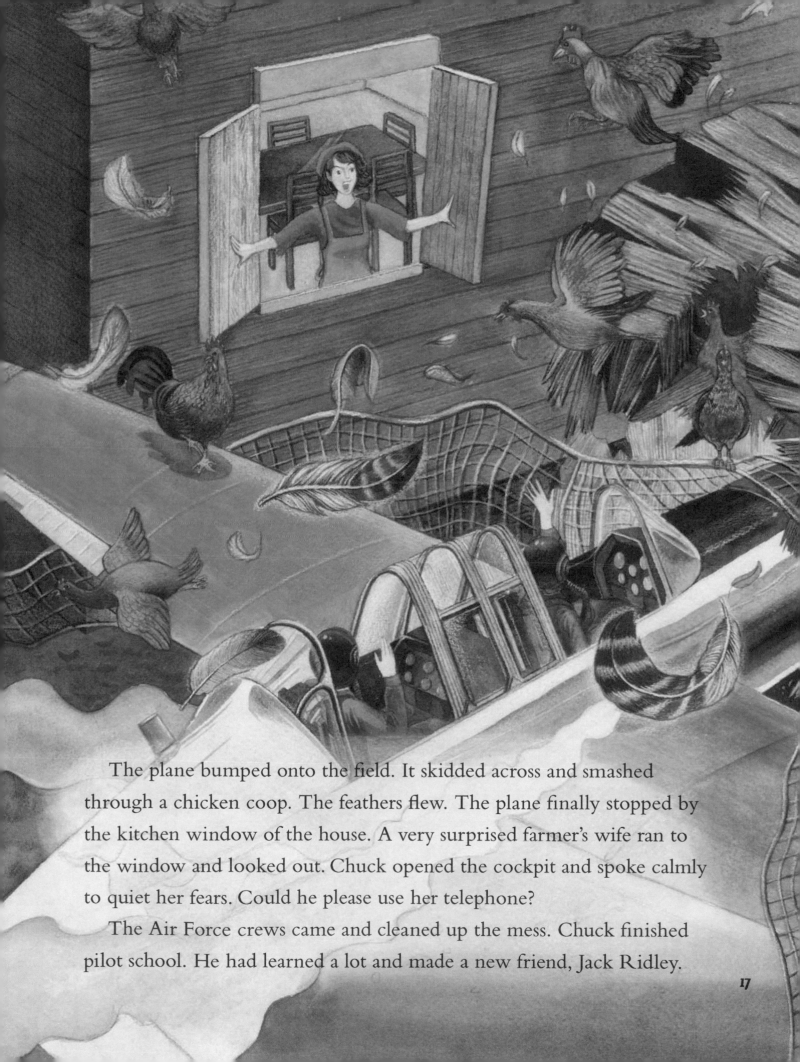

The plane bumped onto the field. It skidded across and smashed through a chicken coop. The feathers flew. The plane finally stopped by the kitchen window of the house. A very surprised farmer's wife ran to the window and looked out. Chuck opened the cockpit and spoke calmly to quiet her fears. Could he please use her telephone?

The Air Force crews came and cleaned up the mess. Chuck finished pilot school. He had learned a lot and made a new friend, Jack Ridley.

17

Chapter Four ★ How Sound Works

Chuck needed to understand how sound works. A good place to begin thinking about sound is to imagine a pond of water and a bridge over it. Suppose you walk out on the bridge and drop a rock into the pond. What do you see in the water? You see a ripple go out from the splash. It is a round circle. And it goes out from where the rock splashed.

Sound works very much like that ripple in the water. We are all living in a pond of air. The air can have ripples just like the water. Think about your teacher standing in front of the class. She claps her hands and a ripple goes out just like when the rock drops into the pond of water.

When this ripple reaches the first row of students, they hear the clap. This happens quickly because the ripple is moving at the speed of sound.

Then it travels to the second row and they hear the clap.

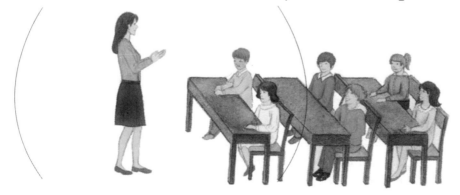

It keeps on traveling. If a child lived a mile from the school, it would take about five seconds for that sound to reach their house. Of course, the teacher would have to clap hard to be heard so far away.

Imagine an airplane on the runway ready to take off. Like the teacher's clap, its engine sends out waves. But unlike a single hand clap, the engine's sound keeps coming. It actually sends out thousands of ripples per second.

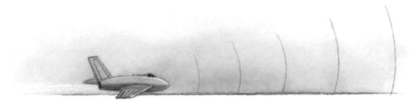

When the airplane takes off, it begins to chase the sound waves that it is creating. The waves are going forward, but the plane is quickly coming after them.

Now think about the plane when it flies nearly as fast as the sound waves. It will be making more ripples as it goes and they will be building up in front of it. The ripples go forward at the speed of sound. But the plane is going forward nearly as fast, chasing those ripples as it makes more. The ripples cannot get away from the plane and they keep building up. They build and build and form a huge pressure wave in front of the plane. This is called the SOUND BARRIER.

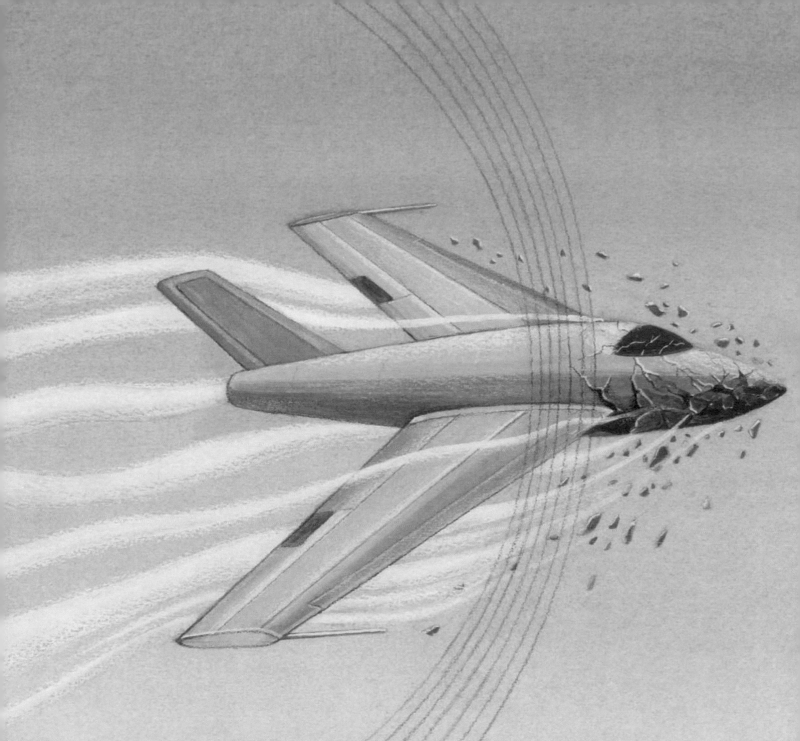

In the 1940s, people believed that planes should not go faster than the speed of sound. The huge pressure wave would smash them to pieces. When the British pilot Geoffrey De Havilland, Jr. flew near the speed of sound, his special flying wing test airplane broke up and crashed. The British ended that testing.

Chapter Five ★ The X-1 Rocket Ship

In 1947, Colonel Boyd told Chuck that a new rocket plane called the X-1 was being designed to break through the sound barrier. He reminded Chuck of how risky it would be. Then he asked if he would like to be the pilot. Chuck said yes. He asked Chuck if he could name a backup pilot. Chuck named Bob Hoover. He asked Chuck for a really smart person to be flight engineer. Chuck chose Jack Ridley.

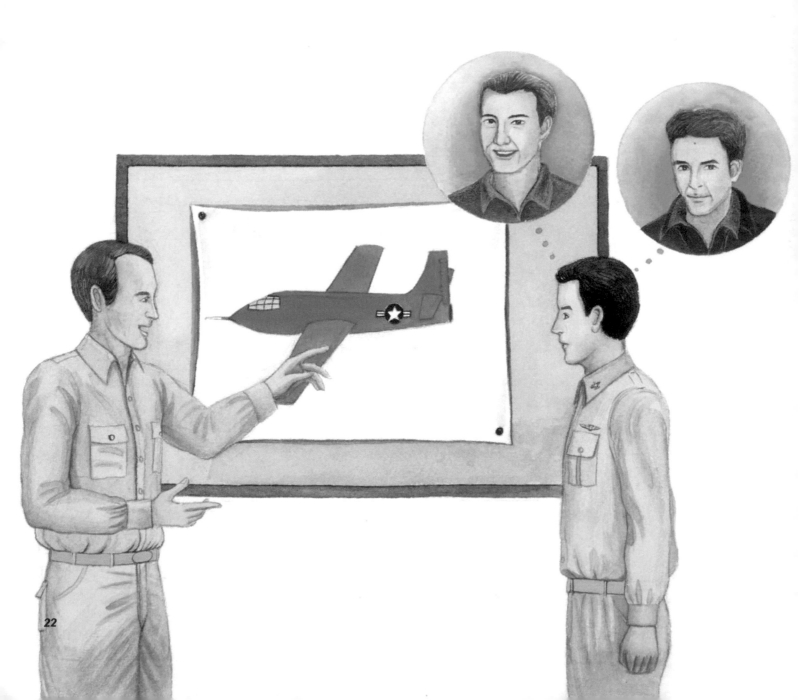

Chuck, Bob, and Jack flew to Muroc Air Base on the Mojave Desert in California where the new rocket plane was to be tested.

The X–1 had rocket engines that burned fuel so fast that they would run out of it in three or four minutes. The rocket plane did not carry enough fuel to take off, climb high in the sky, and run tests. How could they get up in the air without wasting fuel? The crew hooked the X–1 to the bottom of a large bomber. The bomber took off and did not drop the X–1 until it was high enough to begin the tests.

As they took off, Chuck and Jack rode in the bomber. Chuck was ready to climb into the X–1 when they were high enough to perform the tests. Bob flew behind them in a chase plane to watch the X–1 fly and to check constantly to make sure there were no problems.

When they flew high enough, Chuck climbed down into the X–1. Because the space was so small, the door was a separate piece that had to be attached. Jack handed Chuck the X–1 door. After the door was closed and locked, Chuck called the bomber pilot and said he was ready.

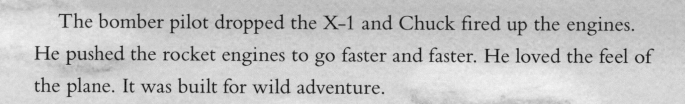

The bomber pilot dropped the X-1 and Chuck fired up the engines. He pushed the rocket engines to go faster and faster. He loved the feel of the plane. It was built for wild adventure.

Every time Chuck flew, people on the ground came to watch. They wanted to see the X-1 fly faster than sound.

One day Chuck decided to give them a show. He turned off his engines and quietly dove towards the airport. Just as he crossed the runway, he turned on the four engines full blast. He zoomed past them with a roar. He pointed the X-1 towards the sky. He flew straight up for seven miles at 560 miles per hour. Those people had never before seen a rocket plane with such power.

Chapter Six ✪ Flying Near the Speed of Sound

Each test flight pushed the X-1 to a faster speed and the next one was planned for 620 miles per hour. Now they were getting close to the speed of sound, which is 660 miles per hour when you are high in the sky. Though this speed was risky, Chuck was looking forward to the flight.

The X-1 was taken up and dropped again from the bomber in the usual way. But when it came close to 620 miles per hour, it began to shake and to bump. Chuck could hear rough air rumbling outside the plane. He pulled back on his control wheel to slow down. But nothing happened. His control wheel had stopped working. His plane would not respond. Was he going to crash?

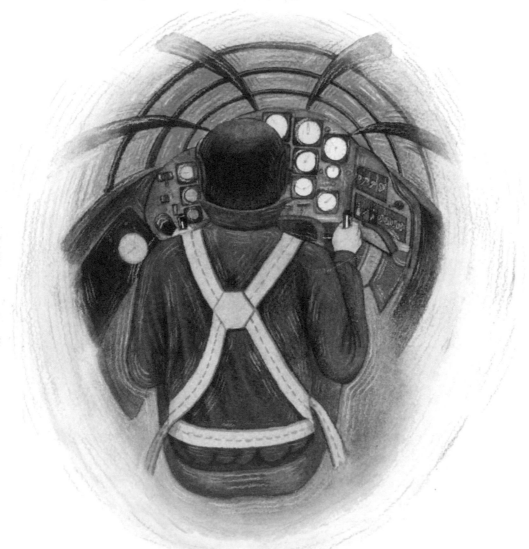

Quickly he turned off the engines so that the plane would slow and he could, once again, fly normally. After all of these flights, it seemed that the X-1 testing was over. It could not be controlled at 620 miles per hour. Chuck glided the plane back for a landing.

He explained to Bob and Jack what had happened. They gathered the crew and talked about the flight. It appeared that the X-1 would not be able to fly faster than sound.

But Jack Ridley went off by himself. He computed some numbers and read more information about the X-1.

Jack hurried back to the group and explained what he had discovered. There was a special tail adjustment on the X-1. It might help Chuck fly faster and control the plane better.

Chuck went up for another flight. He pushed the X-1 to 620 miles per hour. The plane began to shake and to bump. His control wheel stopped working again. This time Chuck tried the special tail control. It worked. He could steer perfectly even with the bumping and shaking. He headed his plane back to the landing field, ready to tell everyone the good news.

But before he could tell them, the windows started to ice. Usually, he could wipe it away, but the freezing was worse this time. Chuck could not see. He tried to scratch off the ice, but more was forming. He radioed Richard Frost in the chase plane to say that he was flying blind.

Richard told Chuck that he would get him home. Chuck did whatever Richard said. Bank left. Straighten out. Wheel forward a bit. Bank left again. Richard told him all the moves until he landed safely at the airport.

Chuck was very tired that weekend and went home to get some rest. After dinner one night, he and his wife borrowed two horses to go riding in the hills. They had a quiet evening on the desert and then turned back.

Chuck decided to race his wife home. He rode very fast.

But in the dark, Chuck could not see that someone had closed the gate. He crashed into it and fell off his horse. He injured his chest and back.

Chapter Seven ★ Broken Ribs and Still Flying

Chuck went to the doctor. His whole body hurt. The doctor said he had cracked two ribs and taped up his chest. He might have to stop flying. It hurt so much to move his arms that he couldn't lift anything. Would this be the end of his high speed flights?

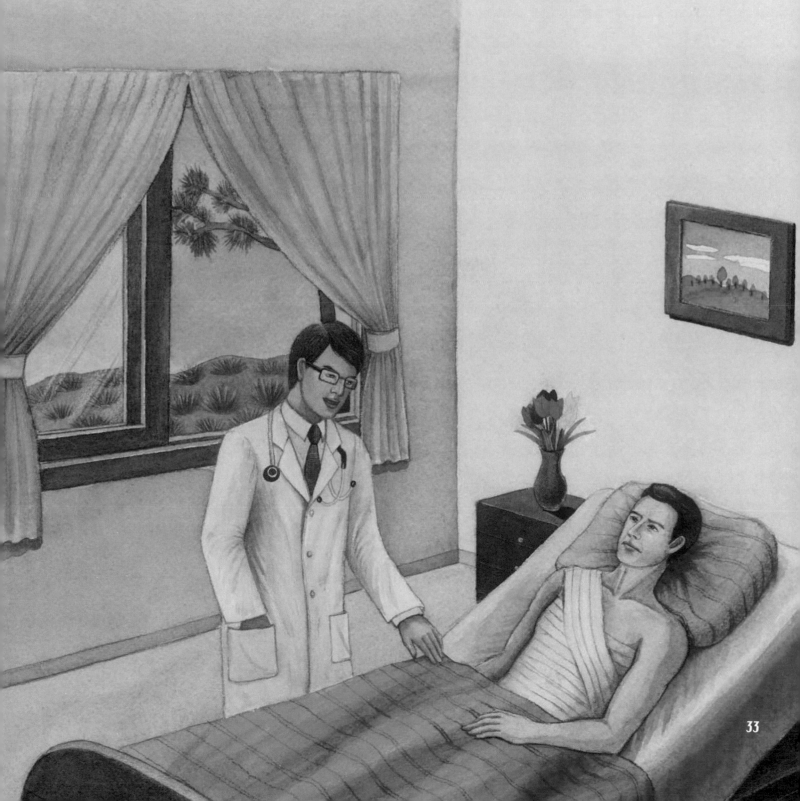

Chuck went to the airfield and talked to Jack about his pain. Yes, he was able to climb into the cockpit. Yes, he could move the controls. But he could not close and lock the heavy door. Chuck would not be able to fly with such severe injuries.

Then Jack had an idea. He sawed off a broomstick handle. He told Chuck that if he held the stick in his left hand, he could reach across to lock the door. Yes, Chuck would use the broom handle. Because of Jack's smart idea, he would be able to fly.

The X–1 was loaded onto the bomber. They took off and Chuck entered the X–1. This time he was supposed to go even faster, but he had never flown with broken ribs before. And what if the plane became uncontrollable at the new higher speed? Also, there could be other surprises out there waiting for him.

He pushed his plane out to 620 miles per hour. As expected, the X–1 shook. But with the extra tail control, Chuck was able to fly straight. He was being very careful because any second something could go wrong.

He flew the plane even faster. What is that? The speedometer needle was jumping wildly. It went back and forth. It went off the scale. Chuck pushed the speed faster still.

Then he radioed Jack in the bomber and told him that his speedometer was acting funny. Jack laughed and told Chuck it was his imagination.

Chuck laughed too, but still he wondered what was wrong.

The X-1 flight was suddenly smooth. The plane was flying beautifully.

Then the engineers on the ground heard a huge boom. Chuck had broken the sound barrier! He had just gone supersonic!

The speed of sound is often called Mach 1.0 and he had just flown to Mach 1.07 or about 700 miles per hour.

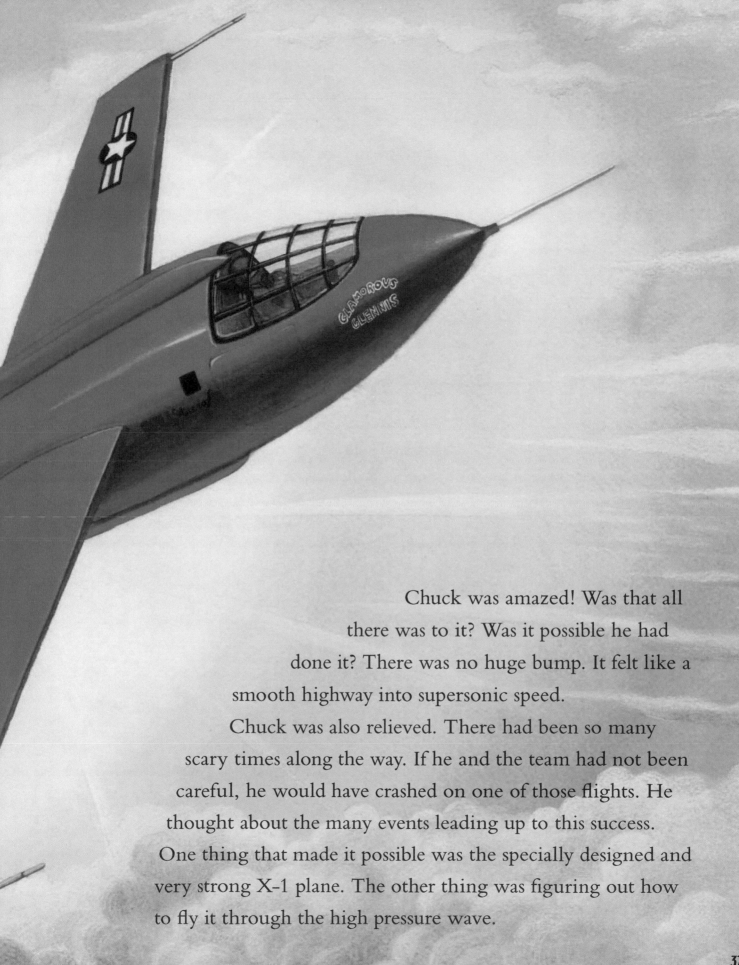

Chuck was amazed! Was that all there was to it? Was it possible he had done it? There was no huge bump. It felt like a smooth highway into supersonic speed.

Chuck was also relieved. There had been so many scary times along the way. If he and the team had not been careful, he would have crashed on one of those flights. He thought about the many events leading up to this success. One thing that made it possible was the specially designed and very strong X–1 plane. The other thing was figuring out how to fly it through the high pressure wave.

After landing, everyone wanted to celebrate and spread the good news. But the Air Force said they must keep the flight a secret. They did not want other countries to find out right away what the U. S. Air Force had done. So Chuck's crew went to his house and had a private party.

Chapter Eight ★ Hero

Chuck's success was announced several months later. He had broken the sound barrier on October 14, 1947 and become a national hero. He was given an award by the President of the United States, President Harry Truman.

The famous news magazine, *Time,* put Chuck on the cover and told the whole X-1 story.

Chuck was invited to give many speeches. He told people how much he loved flying. He told about the sound barrier and breaking it. He told how his many years of hard work had led to his success. Now airplane companies knew how to build planes that could fly faster than sound. In the years that followed, many of them were built. Chuck's achievement had taken aviation into the supersonic age.

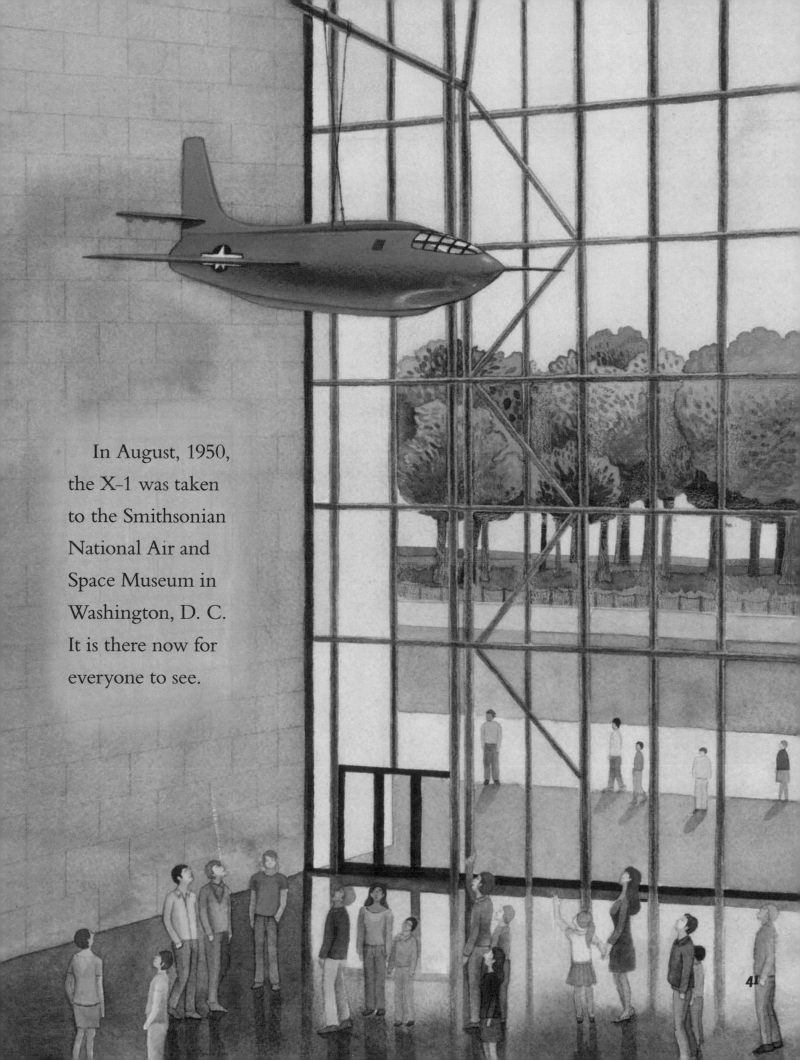

In August, 1950, the X–1 was taken to the Smithsonian National Air and Space Museum in Washington, D. C. It is there now for everyone to see.

41

Chuck continued his life as an Air Force pilot. He tested more than 180 planes over the years. Chuck Yeager still loved to fly airplanes.

Glossary

CHASE PLANE When one airplane is being tested, another plane often flies near it so that its pilot can watch the test plane. The chase plane pilot can sometimes help the test plane pilot by telling what he sees. For example, if the test plane is smoking or there is a fuel leak, the chase plane pilot can tell the test pilot and the crew on the ground what he sees. That can help them understand what is happening in the test.

COLONEL BOYD Colonel is a very high rank in the U. S. Air Force. It is pronounced "kernel" like a kernel of corn. Chuck Yeager's boss was the very strict and demanding Colonel Albert G. Boyd who is usually called just Colonel Boyd.

CONTROL STICK The main control in some airplanes is the "control stick." It is a large lever that comes up from the floor of the cockpit just in front of the pilot's seat. If you push the stick forward, the airplane nose goes down and the plane begins to dive. If you pull the stick back, the nose goes up and you begin to climb. If you lean the stick towards the right, the whole plane will lean towards the right so that you can turn right. Leaning the stick towards the left will enable the plane to turn left. The pilot also uses rudder pedals in turns.

CONTROL WHEEL If there is no control stick, the main control on the airplane is a "control wheel." It is like the steering wheel on automobiles. But on a plane, you can push the wheel forward and the nose will go down. You will begin to dive. You can pull the wheel back and the nose will go up. You will begin to climb. Turning the wheel left or right causes the plane to lean either left or right for the purpose of doing a turn. The pilot also uses rudder pedals in turns.

DOGFIGHT In the 1940's, a plane would shoot down another plane by sneaking up behind and firing its guns. But if the other guy saw him coming, he could turn very hard and try to get a shot at the plane that was approaching. Then the approaching plane would turn hard to re-aim at the other plane. They would chase after each other in a tangle of wild twists and turns.

FLIGHT ENGINEER The flight engineer knows much about airplanes and test flying. He computes how much fuel will be needed, the velocities and altitudes of the tests, and how the plane should be flown. If something goes wrong, his job is to figure out what happened and how to fix it.

JET ENGINE Jet engines were invented in the 1940's. Unlike previous planes, jet planes have no propeller on the front. They suck air into the front of the engine and burn fuel in the rushing air. This causes the air to stream out the rear of the engine at very high speeds. It pushes the plane forward.

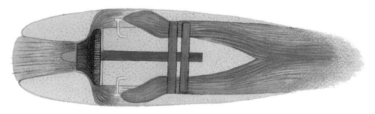

MACH 1.0 A term used to indicate the speed of sound, which is 660 miles per hour at test altitude. The number following the word "Mach" refers to how much faster or slower a speed is in relation to the speed of sound. For instance, Mach 0.5 means half the speed of sound (330 miles per hour at altitude) and Mach 2.0 means twice the speed of sound (1320 miles per hour at altitude). When Chuck broke the sound barrier, he flew Mach 1.07 or about 700 miles per hour. Near the ground, the speed of sound is about 760 miles per hour.

MUROC AIR BASE An air base on the Mojave Desert in California. It later became Edwards Air Force Base.

PROPELLER In many airplanes, the engines are similar to those in automobiles. Large fan blades are attached to the front of the engine and they are called the propeller. The engine spins the propeller at high speeds to pull the plane forward.

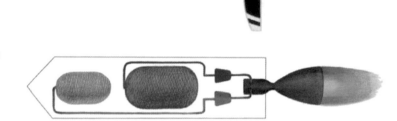

ROCKET ENGINE A different kind of engine for pushing a plane forward is a "rocket" engine. This is similar to a jet engine in that it burns fuel which causes a huge rush of air out the rear of the engine. That rush of air pushes the plane forward. Unlike a jet engine, the rocket engine does not have an air intake at the front. It brings along its own oxygen in tanks just as it brings along fuel. Rocket engines were used in the X-1 because they were much more powerful than jet engines. But they ran out of fuel after just three or four minutes of flight.

SOUND BARRIER This is explained in Chapter Four. If a plane flies so fast that it almost catches up with its own sound waves, a huge pressure wave builds up in front of its nose. This pressure wave is called the "sound barrier" and it can damage a plane that is not well constructed.

SUPERSONIC When an airplane bursts through the sound barrier, it is said to have gone "supersonic." It is flying faster than the speed of sound. The process of bursting through the barrier causes a huge boom, called the "sonic boom," that can be heard for miles. Modern passenger airliners do not fly supersonic. The only exception was the British-French plane called the Concorde. But that type of airplane has been retired. Many military planes can go supersonic.

U. S. AIR FORCE The United States has many soldiers to defend our country. Some soldiers fight on the ground and most of them are in the U. S. Army or Marines. Some soldiers fight on ships out at sea. They are mostly in the U. S. Navy. Some soldiers fight in airplanes. They are mostly in the U. S. Air Force.

Readings

★

Ayres, Carter M., *Chuck Yeager, Fighter Pilot,* Lerner Publications Company, 1988.

Freeze, Di, *In the Cockpit with Chuck Yeager,* Kindle Edition, 2012.

Gaffney, Timothy R., *Chuck Yeager, First Man to Fly Faster than Sound,* Regensteiner Publishing Enterprises, Inc., 1986.

Hoover, R. A. "Bob" and Mark Shaw, *Forever Flying: Fifty Years of High-Flying Adventures,* Simon and Schuster, Inc., 1996.

Levinson, Nancy Smiler, *Chuck Yeager: The Man Who Broke the Sound Barrier,* Walker Publishing Company, Inc., 1988.

Martin, Michael J., *The Importance of Chuck Yeager,* Lucent Books, 2003.

Pisano, Dominick A., F. Robert van der Linden, and Frank H. Winter, *Chuck Yeager and the Bell X-1: Breaking the Sound Barrier,* Harry N. Abrams, Inc., 2006.

Stein, R. Conrad, *Chuck Yeager Breaks the Sound Barrier,* Children's Press, 1997.

Williams, Colleen Madonna Flood, *Chuck Yeager,* Chelsea House Publishers, 2003.

Yeager, Chuck and Leo Janos, *Yeager, An Autobiography,* Bantam Books, Inc., 1985.

Yeager, Chuck and Charles Leerhsen, *Press On: Further Adventures in the Good Life,* Bantam Books, Inc., 1988.

Yeager, Chuck and Bob Cardenas, Bob Hoover, Jack Russell, James Young, *The Quest for Mach One: A First Person Account of Breaking the Sound Barrier,* Penguin Putnam, Inc., 1997.

The Story Behind the Story of

Chuck Yeager Goes Supersonic

General Chuck Yeager was born in 1923 and grew up in rural Hamlin, West Virginia during the Great Depression. The economic hard times brought many responsibilities to Chuck on his family farm when he was young. This probably did much to develop his dedication and strong work ethic.

Chuck graduated from high school just as World War II began and he signed up to join the Army Air Corps. As soon as he discovered there were opportunities for young men to learn to fly, he pursued that option. In earlier times, flying had been reserved for army officers, but the needs of the war opened up this possibility for lower ranks. Chuck spent some months as an aircraft mechanic and then went on to flight training.

After this training, he went to England to fly P-51 fighter planes against the Germans. He was shot down over France early in his tour of duty and the French underground heroically saved him and helped him to escape to Spain and back to England. There he was told that he would have to return to the U. S. because the policy was to not let pilots return to combat who had familiarity with the French underground. If they were captured again, it might result in the release of confidential information about the underground. But Chuck wanted to continue to fight and argued his case all the way to the commander, General Dwight D. Eisenhower at the Supreme Headquarters, who gave his approval for Chuck to fly more missions.

He returned to fighter duty and was credited with many successful engagements by the time he finished his tour.

Upon returning to the United States, he married his long time sweetheart, Glennis, and in the years that followed, they had four children. Chuck had named his P-51 fighter during the war after her, Glamorous Glen, and a similar name, Glamorous Glennis, would later go on the record breaking Bell X-1.

Chuck's first assignment in the U. S. was at Wright-Patterson Air Force Base at Dayton, Ohio where he was given the duties of a maintenance pilot. Here he had the opportunity to fly air shows and he met Bob Hoover who would be a very important partner in his many exploits. Chuck showed off his very special talent for getting ailing planes home after they began to have problems of one kind or another. Occasionally after an air show, a pilot would leave the plane behind and return home without it because there were so many problems with those early jets. Chuck was often asked to bring the planes home. He probably caught the attention of his superiors because of his unusual flying abilities and instincts for how to manage a plane with mechanical problems.

Test pilots in those days usually had college degrees so it was unexpected that a person without such training would get to go to test pilot school. Fortunately for Chuck, he was able to make friends with the apparent genius, Jack Ridley, who helped him along the way. Chuck was certainly not a natural choice to fly the high profile X-1 plane since he was so young and had less experience than many of the existing test pilots who also had college degrees. He was only twenty-four years old when he began the

1903	1923	1927	1943	1947	1953	1958	1962	1966
	Chuck Yeager is born		Chuck enters WWII as fighter pilot		Jackie Cochran is the first woman to break the sound barrier		Chuck becomes commander of Aerospace Research Pilot School	
Wright brothers first powered flight		Charles Lindbergh flies across the Atlantic Ocean		Chuck breaks the sound barrier in the X-1		The supersonic fighter F-104 becomes operational		Chuck goes to Philippines during Vietnam war

famous X-1 flights. This led to some professional jealousy for those more experienced fliers and, for some of them, maybe the hope that Chuck would fail. When the X-1 flights began, he had an impulse one day to show those doubters that he could really fly that bird. He did his famous dive at the airstrip and blasted his way across the field and into a spectacular vertical climb as described in the text. (This break from regular testing procedures earned him a sharp rebuke from Colonel Boyd.)

The X-1 testing was at Muroc Air Base on an inland desert in southern California. This base was located on a flat, dry lake bed so that test pilots could land almost anywhere over an eight mile stretch if they had an emergency. This was the initial installation that later became Edwards Air Force Base.

Breaking the sound barrier was a very risky undertaking and others had died when their planes had approached those high speeds. In the early years of the P-38 plane, there had been some unexplained crashes after high speed dives and it needed investigation. So a technical director in the Army decided to go up in a P-38 to study the problem. He dove the P-38, he achieved the high speed, his elevator flap stopped working, his whole plane began to shake violently, his controls froze, and only after a terrible struggle did he avoid death. The reason why Chuck could easily save himself when he lost elevator control was because he was flying horizontally and he could cut his rocket power and slow down to controllable speed. Just a year before Chuck's heroic success, Geoffrey de Havilland, Jr. of the British de Havilland aircraft company lost his life when he pushed their experimental plane, called the Swallow, near the speed of sound and it disintegrated. The Bell engineers who designed the X-1 deserve plenty of credit for installing a completely moveable horizontal stabilizer so when the regular elevator failed, the pilot could move the whole stabilizer.

The horse riding accident might seem unimportant in this story. But if the Air Force doctors had known that Chuck was partially disabled, one can assume that they would have grounded him and made a decision to get another pilot or wait for him to recover. But he went forward in his usual brash manner and flew the critical barrier-crashing flight anyway.

His wild experiences were not over and, in the years that followed, he did a lot of risky flying to test later planes. In 1962, he was appointed to be commandant of the new Aerospace Research Pilots School that was being created at Edwards. Later, Chuck became a wing commander and headed the 405th Fighter Wing that fought in Vietnam. He was promoted to the rank of Brigadier General in 1969 and retired in 1975.

General Chuck Yeager lost Glennis to cancer in 1990 and now lives with his second wife, Victoria, in Penn Valley, California.

			The British-French supersonic airliner Concorde and the		Chuck flies an F-15 through the sound barrier to celebrate
Neil Armstrong walks on the moon		Chuck retires from the Air Force	supersonic fighters F-15 and F-16 become operational		the 65th anniversary of his historic flight in the X-1
1969	**1974**	**1975**	**1976**	**1985**	**2012**
	Supersonic F-14 becomes operational		Chuck receives Congressional Medal of Honor	President Ronald Reagan awards Chuck the Presidential Medal of Freedom	Felix Baumgartner freefalls 833.9 mph, making him the first person to break the sound barrier without an aircraft

Acknowledgments

We look forward to delivering the story of our daring American hero to the next generation. We thank Dr. Stephanie M. Smith, Historian at the Air Force Flight Test Center, for detailed comments on our coverage and have tried to incorporate her ideas properly. We are indebted to a long list of reviewers in the Society of Children's Book Writers and Illustrators over several years. We especially thank Bonnie Bader and Barbara Younger for their enthusiastic comments and help. We also wish to thank teachers in the local school systems who used earlier versions of the book in their classes and helped us adapt our material to the needs and style of young readers: Ellen Cameron, Nancy Cheek, Sharla Coleman, Daniel Heuser and Karoline Mathewson.

Our editor and advisor for this book has been Susie Wilde. We are very appreciative of her sensitivity and creativity when it comes to language and story telling. We also thank our dear book designer, Julia Gignoux of Freedom Hill Design, for both her artistic taste in book design and her good sense about publishing. Her many contributions have greatly improved this book.

About the Author With a father in the airplane propeller business, Alan Biermann spent a lot of time around airplanes in his early years. During high school and college, he worked in the factory each summer assembling propellers for single and twin engine aircraft. Later he became a sailplane pilot and flew many flights over the Mojave Desert near where Captain Yeager had broken the sound barrier. Then he spent his career as a professor of computer science, mostly at Duke University, and wrote a textbook that has been used widely throughout the United States and abroad. When his children, especially his son, reached the early-reader stage, they very badly wanted to read *real* stories about *real* heroes and few if any could be found at their reading level. He wrote this book to give modern-day early readers a story that his own children would have loved if they had been given the chance.

Alan lives in Chapel Hill, North Carolina with his wife, Alice Gordon. They enjoy very much their two granddaughters, Isabel and Sophia, and their parents who live nearby.

About the Illustrator Yaejin Lim is a painter, illustrator, and art educator. She studied painting, drawing, and illustration at the School of the Art Institute of Chicago and Rhode Island School of Design and art education at Harvard Graduate School of Education. Creating children's books is a perfect way for her to employ her artistic talent and passion for art education. Yaejin lives in Pasadena, California, with her husband, Alexey Gorshkov. Her website is www.limyaejin.com

Made in the USA
Charleston, SC
05 February 2013